Unstoppable

My Journey Through Adversity

Written By

Lemmesha Wilbert

Copyright © 2025 by Lemmesha

All rights reserved. No part of this publication may be reproduced, distributed, or transmitted in any form or by any means—electronic, mechanical, photocopying, recording, or otherwise—without the prior written permission of the author, except in the case of brief quotations used in reviews or articles.

This book is a true account of my personal experiences. For privacy and respect, the names of certain individuals and identifying details have been changed. Any resemblance to actual persons, living or dead, is purely coincidental.

Cover design by **Mark Watson**

Ebook ISBN:
Paperback ISBN: 978-1-917766-51-7
Hardcover ISBN: 978-1-917766-52-4

First Edition
For information, contact:
Lifted Visionz LLC
liftedvisionz@outlook.com

Table of Contents

Introduction 1
Early Childhood 2
Teenage Years 6
Early Adulthood 10
The Final Straw 35
    The Unraveling: Late 2018 – Early 2020 35
    Rebuilding Broken Ties 49
    Watching Death Up Close 57
    The Weight of an Impossible Decision 65
    Breaking the News to Our Children 67
    Saying Goodbye 68
    Support in the Darkness 70
    A New Facility, Closer to Home 91
    The Day I'll Never Forget 101
    The Aftermath of Truth 115
Closing Chapter 123
Reflection on Life Now 126
Acknowledgments 129
About the Author 130
Preview for the Next Journey 131

Introduction

This is my story—a journey of love, loss, resilience, and survival. It's a story of breaking generational curses, navigating heartbreak, and finding strength in the face of unimaginable pain. I dedicate this book to my sister Amina, who passed away on October 18, 2022. Amina was more than just my sister; She'd often tell me, 'Your story has the power to inspire and heal others.' Her unwavering faith in me gave me the courage to keep writing. This book is for her, and for anyone who has ever felt like giving up but chose to keep going.

Early Childhood

I was born and raised on the EastSide of San Jose, CA, a community where everyone knew each other. As a little girl, I loved to read. It became my sanctuary, my escape from the turbulent chaos of life at home. My family was small—just me, my mom (Marie), my older brother (Malcolm), who often drifted away, and my younger brother (Zayden), who came into our lives later. My father (Marcus) was absent during my childhood years, leaving my mom to navigate the challenges of single parenthood, and she did her best to provide a stable home.

But life wasn't without its darkest moments. Between the ages of 7 and 9, I endured abuse at the hands of my cousin Terrance—an experience no child should ever have to bear. Despite the stability my mom fought to maintain, dark shadows loomed over my early years.

I stayed silent for years, carrying the weight of that pain alone. Those years left deep scars, but they also taught me the power of reclaiming my voice, a lesson that continues to shape who I am today.

Unstoppable: My Journey Through Adversity

At the age of nine, my world was turned upside down. At the time, my mom, my baby brother Zayden, and I were staying with my grandparents. We had moved back to San Jose, CA, from Fairfield after a troubling incident forced my mom to uproot our lives. Life felt uncertain, but my mom did everything possible to shield us from it. However, years of underlying tensions between my mom and my grandmother (Nicole) escalated into a fierce dispute, leading to my mom's arrest.

In that moment, our lives fractured as if the ground beneath us had crumbled. Zayden and I found ourselves in a children's shelter, an unfamiliar place we'd call home for months. I was eventually sent to a foster home, but it felt foreign and unwelcoming, and I soon returned to the shelter.

During that turbulent time, Zayden and I were placed in separate foster homes in Santa Cruz, CA. The separation was heart-wrenching, but I made it a point to visit him frequently, offering what little support I could as I struggled to cope with my own sense of disconnection. Those visits were a fragile lifeline, a reminder of our bond amidst the chaos.

As I navigated this new reality, I made a few friends, but my coping mechanisms were fragile, and I began acting out—lying and stealing. It was a desperate attempt to regain control in a world that seemed determined to upend me.

Eventually, the time came for me to live with my father permanently. I felt a mix of relief, happiness, and sadness as I said goodbye to Zayden. Though we'd be apart, I knew I'd still see him during visitations, and my mom would join us, accompanied by my grandfather.

A few months later, we received devastating news: it would be our last visit because my brother was moving to Texas. The day we said goodbye was heartbreaking. Not long after, I found out he had been adopted, and all contact with him was lost. I vowed to find him when I got older, and that promise stayed with me for years. I spent countless hours searching, driven by the hope that we could one day be reunited.

Moving in with my father wasn't just about starting fresh—it meant stepping into a whole new family dynamic. My younger brother (Marcus II) and my bonus mom (Lauren)—who I don't consider a stepmother but rather a second mother—were also part of the household. Adjusting to this new life wasn't easy at first. Lauren and I clashed often; our disagreements filled the house with tension, making even small interactions feel strained. But everything started to change one day when she made homemade macaroni and cheese. It might sound funny, but yes, food really can bring people together! That small act of kindness opened the door to a stronger bond between us, and over time, we grew closer.

Even with the new stability, I was still rebellious. Though I had left stealing behind, dishonesty still clung to me, and my grades told their own story of struggle. Adjusting to a new school system proved challenging, and my grades reflected that. During this time, I also had the chance to meet another sibling—my younger sister (Jalissa). Jalissa and I bonded instantly, and as I embraced my expanding family, I discovered I had an older brother, Malcolm, along with two younger brothers, Zayden and Marcus II. Building these relationships was meaningful to me, and they became a source of joy and strength.

Teenage Years

As I adjusted to my new school and surroundings, I started forming friendships. One friend, in particular, stood out, and we became thick as thieves. If you saw one of us, you saw the other. My junior high years were filled with routine—classes, friendships, and small adventures—but high school opened doors to new opportunities and unexpected challenges.

I started high school at John F. Kennedy High School in Fremont, CA, where I was living at the time. It was an incredible experience. I loved everything about it—the diversity, the sense of community, and the friendships I formed. I joined the Black Student Union, immersed myself in photography, and even wrote a short film that captured my journey and personal growth. But my time there was cut short during my sophomore year when I learned we were moving. I was devastated. Leaving my best friend Shay and the relationships I had built was heartbreaking.

We moved to Lancaster, CA, a town that was still being developed. I finished my sophomore year at Quartz Hill

High School, where my cousin Danae was a familiar face in an otherwise unfamiliar place. While the experience was decent, the school was far from home, and I wanted to transfer somewhere closer.

My final two years of high school were a whirlwind of self-discovery, marked by yet another transfer—this time to Antelope Valley High. Switching between three different schools felt like being thrown into a new world over and over again—new faces, unfamiliar hallways, and the constant sense of being an outsider. At first, I kept to myself, struggling to find my footing. But one day, a simple question from a boy—asking my name—sparked an unexpected friendship. Over time, my social circle grew, mostly with male friends, along with a few close female friends.

I wasn't the kind of girl who made the yearbook's 'Most Popular' list, but I walked the halls like I belonged. My confidence was my shield, even when the world around me tried to chip away at it. My senior year was particularly memorable. I faced an altercation with another girl over a guy I wasn't even dating. It felt like an attempt to derail my graduation, but my two closest friends had my back and wouldn't let that happen. Despite some tensions with other girls, I found that when people approached me with curiosity instead of judgment, meaningful connections could be formed.

I also found solace in my travel choir class, where I explored my love for singing. Like any rebellious teenager, I had my fair share of 'brilliant' ideas—sneaking out, skipping school, and somehow believing I could outwit my parents. Spoiler: I couldn't. But those years taught me the value of accountability and the importance of learning from my choices.

High school provided me with work experience opportunities. Through a school program, I worked at Six Flags during two summers, balancing my job with summer school. Around this time, I first noticed Darius, the man who would later become my husband. We didn't speak then, but I vividly remember him noticing me.

Years later, fate brought us together again—this time through a dating app called Air G Date. To my surprise, he remembered exactly what I was wearing the first time he saw me—down to the green, army-style outfit and black Lugz. At first, we were just acquaintances. He reached out because he wanted my help reconnecting with an on-again, off-again girlfriend from my school. I reluctantly agreed to pass along his message and number, but she never contacted him.

From there, our conversations became more frequent. Eventually, I decided to be bold and told him, "If she doesn't want to talk to you, I will." From that day forward, we talked almost every day, and a deeper connection began to form.

Despite the challenges, my teenage years were filled with lessons, personal growth, and relationships that would shape my future.

Lemmesha

Early Adulthood

After high school, I landed my first job at Victoria's Secret. However, Before I even started, my life took an unexpected turn—I found out I was pregnant. This revelation led to being kicked out of the house by my father who gave me an ultimatum to get an abortion or leave his home. I chose to leave. From that day forward I had not seen my father for 1yr and a half. I still communicated with him on special days and occasions. My bonus mom, Lauren, was so disappointed in me that she told me nothing I did would ever work. Her words forced me to find a new path forward. Unsure of what to do, I turned to my biological mother and told her the news. She welcomed me back with open arms, saying she had always known this day would come. She knew, even before I did, that I would return to her.

I moved back in with my mom, and for the next year and a half, I adjusted to a new chapter in my life. However, settling back into familiar surroundings came with an unexpected challenge. My bonus dad, Caleb, had changed the household dynamic, and I struggled to adapt—like a musician learning to play a new melody. At one point, I moved in with my grandmother, Nicole, for about a month before returning to my mom's house. Despite the stability my mom provided, I faced both emotional and physical struggles during my pregnancy, a consequence of the choices I had made.

Among the hardest challenges I faced was the uncertainty surrounding my son's paternity. There was a possibility that another man, not Darius, could be the father. However, I was always upfront about the situation with everyone involved. Darius, despite the uncertainty, didn't care if the child was biologically his or not. He made it clear that he wanted to be there for both me and my son.

During this time, I found ways to support myself. I got a seasonal job at Sears during the holidays, and like many, I relied on TANF (Temporary Assistance for Needy Families). However, I never let that define me. I worked hard for everything I had, determined to provide a good life for my child.

Six months after giving birth to my son, Isaiah, I moved back to Lancaster to be with his father, who was living with his older sister, Kendra. For a few months, things seemed to settle, but soon we found ourselves bouncing between his two sisters' homes—Kendra's in Lancaster and Arielle's in Long Beach. Though I had no personal issues with either of them and always contributed financially, the constant instability took a toll on me.

The breaking point came when my son and I had a knife pulled on us by Kendra's baby daddy. We were put out of the house in the cold, and my son ended up getting sick. That moment was a wake-up call. I rekindle my relationship with Lauren in Lancaster and stayed with her until my son turned one. Unfortunately, we had a disagreement about the father of my child, which led me to move again.

This time, I stayed briefly with Darius's mother, Sabrina, where he was also living. However, she made it clear that she didn't want me there. With nowhere else to turn, I called my mom, Marie, for help. The tension in the house was suffocating, and before long, I knew I had to leave. Without hesitation, my mom, grandmother, and grandfather drove six hours to pick up Isaiah and me. That day, Darius was faced with a choice: stay behind or come with us. He chose to come and live with me and my family in Fairfield, CA.

Our time in Fairfield wasn't without its challenges. Disagreements between Darius and my family created tension. Despite this, we both decided to pursue a future in the Navy. I passed the entrance test, but there were no available positions for me. Darius, however, failed his exam. That failure became the wedge that drove us apart. A heated argument with Caleb was the final straw. As Darius prepared to leave, Caleb's words cut deep: "When you come back, come back as a man." My heart broke, but I knew I couldn't change his decision.

Determined to create a better future, I continued my journey toward joining the military. The Navy eventually referred me to the Army, where I enlisted. Leaving Isaiah behind was one of the hardest decisions I've ever made, but I knew it was necessary to build a stable future for us. When I left, my son was a year and a half old.

Even during the grueling months of training, I never stopped providing for Darius and our son—making sure they had everything they needed, from financial support to emotional reassurance. The distance was hard, but I held onto the hope that one day we could build the strong, united family I had always envisioned. Still, deep down, I knew that things couldn't stay the same. If we were going to move forward, something had to change when I returned home.

Before I graduated from training, I gave Darius an ultimatum. I told him that if he wasn't at the bus stop when

Lemmesha

I got off the plane, I would be leaving with our son and moving out of state. I made it clear that I wasn't going to make things easy for him, especially since he had missed the birth of our son. This was his chance to show that he was ready to step up and be present for our family.

The moment of truth arrived. After months of separation, I was finally headed home, my heart racing with anticipation and fear. As I stepped off the bus, my eyes searched desperately—and then, there he was. Standing at the bus stop, waiting. It was the first time in a long time that he had seen our son, and in that single moment, he made a choice: to fight for our family.

While I had stayed connected to my son through letters and phone calls with my mother, seeing him again in person brought mixed emotions. My mother had ensured that Darius maintained communication with our son while I was away, but the reality of the separation hit hard when I realized my son didn't recognize us as his parents. That moment was devastating—one of the hardest things I've ever experienced.

Guilt and heartbreak overwhelmed me, knowing that even a short separation had created this gap. It hurt more than words could express. But with time, patience, and love, my son came around. Over time, he adjusted, gradually understanding that we were his parents.

This period of reunion wasn't just about reconnecting with my son—it was also about rebuilding our family. Darius' decision to fully embrace our family was a step toward creating the stability and unity I had always wanted for our son.

After returning from training and rebuilding stability and unity for our son, Darius and I both started working part-time at Sears to provide for our growing family. A year later, in 2009, we welcomed our second son (Tristan) into the world. Life felt like it was coming together, and we solidified our commitment by getting married on April 8, 2010. Those early years of marriage were filled with love, challenges, and a deep desire to create the best life possible for our children.

Four months after our wedding, an unexpected turn of events forced us to relocate to Sacramento, where we spent the next two years adjusting to a new reality. During that time, we took in two of his younger siblings (Deliah & Sarah) and cared for them along with our boys. It was a challenging adjustment, but we did our best to provide a loving home for everyone.

In 2012, we made the decision to move to Merced, hoping the smaller town would offer more space and a fresh start for our growing family. That year brought a mix of joy and sorrow. While Darius' siblings eventually went their separate ways to live with other family members, I found out I was pregnant with our third child (Selena). In the same month I gave birth to our daughter, I lost my uncle (Dale). Losing him was devastating, especially knowing how much he meant to my son. That bittersweet time of welcoming new life while mourning a loss was one of the hardest moments of my life.

As the months went by, we realized that while Merced offered more space, it lacked the job opportunities we needed to truly thrive. In 2013, my parents and I decided to move back to Sacramento together, bringing our children along. Since my parents didn't have their own place at the time, we agreed to share a home. It was a way for all of us to save money and support one another. For a while, the arrangement worked well, and life felt stable.

Just before the move, we experienced another devastating loss—a close friend who was like family to us. The grief of losing someone so dear weighed heavily on us, but we pressed forward, hoping for better days ahead.

Unstoppable: My Journey Through Adversity

In June 2014, Darius lost his favorite person in the world—his grandmother Evelyn. Her passing changed him into a different person someone I had to relearn. The bond they shared was irreplaceable, and losing her left a void in his heart that he carried with him.

No more than six months later, in January 2015, tragedy struck my family as well. My uncle Derek my father's brother was shot and killed in his mother's driveway. It was the most devastating loss I had ever experienced, and it shook my family to its core. My uncle's death left an emptiness that we struggled to fill.

As if fate hadn't already dealt me enough heartache, in June 2015, I lost my grandfather, Wayne, from my mother's side. Losing two family members in the same year, combined with Darius's grief over his grandmother Gigi's passing the year before, felt like an unbearable weight. Grief kept knocking at our door, refusing to give us a moment of peace. These losses weighed heavily on both of us—Darius carried the deep sorrow of losing his grandmother, Gigi, while I mourned the two men who had been the foundation of my world.

Despite the heartache, we kept moving forward. In 2015, Darius encouraged me to make new female "friends," something I wasn't entirely comfortable with due to trust issues. Eventually, I became close with three neighbors (Alyssa, Brianna, & Elise) in our complex, and we formed what felt like meaningful friendships.

By December 2016, however, Brianna and I's friendship took a dark turn. An altercation occurred with Brianna and I who I thought was a friend. I was the godmother of her youngest son and had gone to her apartment because my husband called me. He said she was refusing to return a speaker he had lent her baby daddy (Bishop). When I arrived, I asked her if I can get the speaker, and she agreed that they were right there in the corner of the house. However, as I stepped inside to retrieve it, her sister (Danielle), who was staying with her at the time, sucker-punched me from behind.

I blacked out and lashed out at Danielle's. In the middle of the fight, my husband and her baby daddy pulled me away to prevent me from getting into more trouble, as fighting on the property could result in eviction. Embarrassed by soiling herself, Danielle escalated the situation by grabbing a knife and attempting to stab me. My husband and Brianna's baby daddy pushed me out the door, telling me to go home to avoid further harm.

When I got home, I told my mother what had happened. She immediately went over to confront them, ready to defend my honor. Several neighbors who knew me as a quiet, non-confrontational person came out to support me. They understood that I mostly kept to myself, focusing on work, taking care of my kids, and being a homebody.

That day, my husband and I agreed to let Bishop, the father of her child, stay with us after she kicked him out. Bishop was working with my husband to launch his dream recording company. My husband was thrilled by the opportunity, believing it could secure our family's future, especially since I was the sole provider at the time. In December 2016, I left my job to fully support his vision.

Bishop convinced me to take out a line of credit to help fund the business. Trusting his intentions, I agreed, only to discover later that I had been scammed out of $15,000. Instead of using the money for the business, Bishop funneled it to himself and his baby mama. This betrayal left me in a financial hole, and my husband blamed me for everything that went wrong.

In February 2017, I discovered I was nine weeks pregnant with our fourth child. Around this time, tensions within the household began to rise. My husband became suspicious of me, accusing me of having an affair with

Bishop. Meanwhile, I began to suspect he was entertaining other women. The financial stress, betrayal, and my husband's mistrust pushed me into a dark depression. Losing one car to repossession and being on the verge of losing another compounded the situation. Despite trying to find work, I couldn't hold a job due to my mental state.

By April 2017, the tension with my parents reached a breaking point. I asked them to move out because we weren't seeing eye to eye. Although it was a difficult decision, I felt it was necessary at the time. After they moved, things started to spiral further.

During my pregnancy, I discovered that Alyssa was actually a cousin through marriage. We had been living next door to each other for four years without realizing it. We grew closer, but her sister (Aubrey) and niece (Aria) started visiting our home more often. My husband became particularly close to her sister, which made me uneasy. I wasn't sure how her niece looked up to my husband—whether as a father figure, a brother figure, or something else—but their closeness raised questions for me.

During this period, my husband grew close to a young woman—Elise's goddaughter. She reminded him of his late god sister, and he asked to take on a similar god-brother role with her. Although I tried to trust his intentions, the combination of these relationships added to the tension in our marriage.

In September 2017, I gave birth to our son (Emory), who became my light in the midst of the darkness. He was my saving grace during one of the most difficult periods of my life. After giving birth to our son Emory, Dariuss was nowhere around during my stay at the hospital. Darius claimed to have to get our other children ready for school but that was already taken care of by my brother Malcom and his gf at the time. I fell into postpartum depression due to not having the support of my husband during that time. However, the challenges didn't stop. Aubrey and Aria continued to visit more frequently, supposedly to see the baby, but their actions made me question their motives.

In November 2017, I started working as an independent contractor for Amazon. This was a significant opportunity for me, as I was no longer accustomed to the traditional 9-to-5 lifestyle. Just the thought of working a structured schedule gave me anxiety attacks. Becoming self-employed allowed me the flexibility to set my own hours and, most importantly, be present for my kids without missing out on their lives.

However, balancing work and family wasn't always easy. In hindsight, one of my deepest regrets was being consumed by work. My kids often expressed that I didn't spend enough time with them, and hearing this hurt me to my core. Realizing that my efforts to provide for them came at the cost of missing their most precious moments was heartbreaking.

Despite the challenges, this new venture gave me the freedom to create my own path. I often brought my Alyssa along for the ride, which gave us time to bond and explore Sacramento and surrounding cities we hadn't been familiar with before. These moments strengthened our relationship and brought a sense of joy to the otherwise demanding work.

But while I was out working, things at home began to feel off. My Aubrey and Aria often visited her home without her knowledge while we were out on routes. My husband had been in communication with them, inviting them over while I was away. He enjoyed cooking for them, and of course, they liked to eat.

What unsettled me the most was how he always made it a point to call and inform me that they were at the house so I wouldn't be caught off guard. While his transparency seemed like a good thing, something about the situation still didn't feel right. I couldn't shake the feeling that there was more to their visits than just enjoying a meal.

The Turning Point: January and February 2018

January 16, 2018, is burned into my memory, a day that altered the course of my life forever. I had been working nonstop since giving birth to our son, Emory, four months earlier. That morning, as I was getting ready for work, my husband Darius asked me what time I was leaving and when I would be back. At the time, I dismissed it as a simple concern. But looking back, his question carried a weight I didn't recognize then.

Darius and I already had each other's locations through our phones, so he could easily see where I was at any time. I wasn't working a traditional 9-to-5 job, but the nature of my work allowed me to finish early some days. On this particular day, Alyssa didn't join me like she usually did because she had a meeting to attend.

Lemmesha

I finished my block early and headed home sooner than expected. As I stepped inside, Darius was already waiting at the door, Emory in his arms—as if he'd known I was coming early. As much as I wanted to grab my baby, I couldn't help but notice something off—Darius was sweating profusely, as though he had been exerting himself. When I asked what he had been doing, he casually said he was cleaning up.

But I'm very particular about my home—I have OCD and know when something has been touched or moved. Nothing in the house appeared cleaned, and I didn't smell any cleaning supplies. Before I could even fully step inside, Darius mentioned that Alyssa's sister, Aubrey, was using the hall bathroom.

At first, I didn't think much of it, but something didn't feel right. Normally, Darius would tell me if someone was coming over or already at the house. Why hadn't he done so this time? Feeling uneasy, I dropped my things on the couch by the door and walked out. I headed across the hall to Alyssa's apartment, where she was sitting at the table with her cousin Raven.

I asked Alyssa how long they had been at the apartments, and she told me they'd only arrived about an hour ago.

She thought Aubrey had left, not realizing Aubrey hadn't left—she had gone to my house instead.

Aubrey later came to the apartment, acting as if everything was fine. But it wasn't. That entire night and the following days, I replayed what had happened over and over in my mind, wondering what I could or should have done differently.

On January 19, 2018, I received a message from Aubrey apologizing for coming to my house unannounced while I wasn't home, saying she meant no disrespect. I thanked her and left it at that, but the unease lingered.

Aubrey continued to visit our home occasionally. On February 9, 2018, Aubrey and her daughter Aria came over because Darius had cooked barbecue ribs, which were his specialty and a favorite of many. While Aria and my cousin's daughter, Tandy, were in the kitchen with Darius making plates, Aubrey was outside talking to her boyfriend.

At some point, Aubrey looked through the kitchen window and claimed she saw Darius touch Aria's butt. When she came inside, she confronted him. By this time, I had come out of the back room, where I had been caring for Emory, to find out what was going on.

Aubrey accused Darius of touching Aria inappropriately, but Tandy quickly defended him, saying he had simply moved Aria out of the way with the back of his hand while cleaning up. The situation escalated as what Aubrey claimed and what others said didn't align.

Feeling on edge from the January incident, I couldn't stay silent. I told Aubrey that this had nothing to do with Aria personally, but I brought up what had happened in January and my unresolved feelings about it. Aubrey left with Aria and Tandy and went to Alyssa's apartment to tell her what had happened. I followed shortly after, determined to get answers.

When I arrived, I asked Aria and Tandy directly if Darius had touched her. They both insisted he hadn't and reiterated that he had only moved her out of the way. I explained to Aria that I didn't hold anything against her but needed to address the lingering doubts from the previous incident.

After the dispute, I went home and told Darius to cut all ties with Aubrey and her family. I had a strong feeling that something was brewing, and as his wife, I knew trouble was coming. He assured me he would, but I later discovered he had lied.

On February 11, 2018, another dispute arose. Darius and Aubrey had been discussing the previous incidents, and she told him I had a problem with her, claiming I was talking about her daughter and how she allowed her to dress provocatively. I found out about this through another cousin, who came to me with details about what Aubrey had been saying.

I directly asked Aubrey why she was talking about me to Darius instead of coming to me herself. I also questioned why she involved others who weren't present during the incidents. The conversation turned into a heated exchange, with Aubrey accusing me of disliking her because of my pregnancy hormones and only warming up to her after I had my baby. She accused me of wanting to keep everyone away from Darius. And honestly? She wasn't wrong. How could I trust people who had so openly disrespected me and ignored the fact that he was married?

Darius was just as much at fault, as he did nothing to address or resolve the issues. His refusal to set boundaries with Aubrey and her family only deepened the strain on our marriage.

The Breaking Point: February – July 2018

The sharp buzz of Darius's phone cut through the silence at 4 a.m. in February 24, 2018. I barely stirred. He often had trouble sleeping and would slip out onto the patio to smoke. Nothing unusual. Nothing to question—until an hour later, when my own phone rang. I was too exhausted to get up and check. However, an hour later, at 5 a.m., I received a call that changed everything—Darius had been spotted upstairs with Aria.

Her cousins had seen them together when they arrived to drop off Alyssa's oldest daughter, Tandy. At the time, Alyssa had moved into the apartment above hers. They were spotted on the back side of Alyssa Apartment.

I immediately got up to check, and as I was heading out, Darius walked inside. I asked him where he had been, and without hesitation, he admitted he was with Aria. Shocked, I asked, Why? We had already agreed to cut ties with them. He claimed Aria had texted him—which explained why his phone went off at 4 a.m.—and asked him to come smoke with her, so he went upstairs to do so.

Rage boiled in my chest, but I didn't react. Not yet. I was too drained, too familiar with this cycle of betrayal. What was the point of anger anymore? What would it change?

The following day, February 25, 2018, at 12:24 p.m., I received another message—this time from Autumn (the cousin who spotted Darius and Aria). She was polite and approached me in a way that wasn't meant to cause stress, but her message made it clear that Darius needed to stop talking to Aubrey and Aria. She told me he was wrong for continuing to communicate with them behind my back, especially since their entire family already knew what had happened the day before.

I asked Autumn where she was, and she said she would be over later to talk. I was looking forward to the conversation because I was tired of all the different stories. I wanted everyone in the same room so the truth could finally come out.

At 2:43 p.m., while standing next to my couch with Alyssa and Elise, I received a message that made my stomach drop.

Autumn texted:

Darius needs to keep my name out of his mouth and stop texting Aubrey.

Lemmesha

Also—did he ever mention that he and Aria have been sleeping together?

In your bed.

For about a year.

I literally dropped my phone.

Elise and Alyssa looked at me, stunned, as they could see the shock on my face. Elise picked up my phone, read the message, and her mouth dropped. Alyssa read it next, and her reaction was the same.

Darius happened to walk in at that moment. As soon as he saw the look on our faces, he knew something was wrong. When he saw the message, he immediately became belligerent, yelling that Autumn was lying and that he didn't do any of that.

At this point, I didn't believe him. My gut had been telling me something was off for months, and now all the pieces were falling into place. My mind flashed back to when I had given birth to my son on September 5, 2017.

Aubrey had come to pick up Alyssa from the hospital after I gave birth. I remembered being alone in the hospital from September 5th until I was discharged on September

7th. Darius had claimed he needed to stay home to take care of our other children, but they were already being cared for by my older brother and his girlfriend, who were staying at our place to help get them off to school.

Darius only visited me once—to bring our kids to see me and their new sibling. Other than that, he was nowhere to be found. I had visitors, but the one person who should have been there the entire time was my husband—and he wasn't.

I shut down. I was emotionally disconnected.

The Confrontation – March 2018

On March 1, 2018, I reached out to Aubrey. I wanted everyone in the same room to put everything out in the open, but no one was willing to tell the truth. It was all he said, she said, and I was the one caught in the crossfire, watching my world get turned upside down.

A few weeks passed, and by March 31, 2018, Aubrey left me voice messages with more he-said-she-said drama—this time claiming it was coming from Alyssa.

At this point, I was done.

I had exhausted myself with this situation, and there was no resolution in sight. Even after everything, I still tried to give Aubrey a chance. She asked to see my son, and I had no issue with that. I never dragged my children into adult situations. But apparently, allowing her to see an innocent child made me a "fake friend."

I know what you might be thinking—how dumb could I be? But I wasn't thinking about Aubrey. I was thinking about my children.

Darius and I had been married for eight years at this point, and I wasn't going to throw it all away based on words alone—especially when there were children involved. But I knew something wasn't right. I defended Darius as a wife should, but deep down, my heart and mind were telling me otherwise.

The April Fool's Prank That Wasn't a Prank – April 2018

On April 1, 2018, Aubrey and her cousin Brianna decided to play an April Fool's joke on me.

They called and texted me, saying that Aubrey had slept with Darius and even went so far as to describe intimate details about my body that she shouldn't have known.

Aubrey claimed that Darius had paid her $20 for oral sex and that it had been going on for a while.

I was devastated.

Then, on April 6, 2018, Aubrey reached out again—this time claiming the "prank" was just a test to see who was talking about her behind her back.

I snapped.

I called her every name in the book and told her exactly what she was—a home wrecker who had knowingly entertained a married man. Yes, I blamed Darius, but at that moment, my anger was directed at her.

What hurt even more was that instead of pulling away from Darius, I became more intimate with him. Doubt crept in, whispering cruel questions—was I the reason he turned to someone else? Was I simply... not enough?

On April 7, 2018, Aubrey messaged me again, this time assuming that I had told my kids not to talk to her. But my oldest son, Isaiah, had his own feelings toward her—not because of me. He saw what was happening, and he wasn't blind to the disrespect.

Lemmesha

Then, on April 29, 2018, at 1:30 a.m., as Darius and I were driving home from a birthday party, Aubrey messaged me again—this time about Brianna. She insisted that Brianna was using crystal meth and warned me not to respond if she reached out.

Why she felt the need to tell me this, I had no idea.

That same night, around 9 p.m., Brianna did message me—apologizing for everything and admitting that Aubrey had lied about everything. She confessed that Aubrey had told her secret about her and Darius and had even been making fake pages to contact him.

At that point, I started screenshotting everything. I made sure everyone saw it so no one could twist my words.

The Final Straw

Even after all this, Aubrey continued to reach out for months—even through Elise—until July 2018.

She wanted to convince me it was all a lie, but behind my back, she was telling her family a different story—which, of course, got back to me.

At this point, I was done.

The Unraveling: Late 2018 – Early 2020

A Family Visit & A Major Betrayal (Late 2018)

Toward the end of 2018, Darius's oldest sister, Kendra, along with her daughter, Taliah, and his father, Brandon, visited us. It was the first time any of his family had made the trip to see where we lived. While it was a good visit at first, it didn't last.

Kendra and Taliah left after a few days, but Brandon stayed a bit longer—long enough to witness yet another blowup between me and Darius.

One night, we got into a huge altercation. I was furious and in a moment of anger, I grabbed a stick, ready to hit him. But before I could, he took it from me. He was about to come after me, but my parents and his father stepped in and grabbed him.

With the stick still in his grasp, he lifted it high, his rage seemingly aimed at the TV. But instead of smashing the screen, he turned the fury inward—striking himself in the head.

I was done.

I told him to leave again, and this time, I had a deeper reason—I found out he had been talking to his ex. The same one he was with before me.

He claimed she was getting "marriage advice" from him because she "admired our marriage." But that was a lie.

Darius had asked her for explicit pictures, and she sent them through email—an email he claimed he had no access to.

And that wasn't all. He also had explicit photos from another woman—someone who was supposedly a "friend of the family." A woman who always claimed that Darius was "like a brother" to her.

Just when I thought the chaos had settled, another wave of betrayal crashed over me.

Darius Goes Back to School (2019)

Despite everything, in 2019, Darius decided to go back to school to earn his high school diploma. He wanted to prove to his kids that if he could do it, they could too.

I was proud of him—I had always been proud—but this was a big step for him.

There were times he wanted to give up, but I wouldn't let him.

At school, he quickly made new friends—two women and one man.

At first, I had no issue with it. But over time, things changed.

Darius started referring to them as "sis" and "bro." The friendships got too close, and red flags started appearing.

Lemmesha

I found out that:

- One of the men had a crush on one of the women.
- The other woman was "a lesbian" and jokingly said she would "take me from Darius."

I laughed it off, but my intuition told me something was off.

One day, Darius came home and asked me if he could go to the movies with his three new friends.

And he needed my car to pick them all up.

Now normally, I wouldn't have minded, but something about this didn't sit right.

1. He was married.
2. He didn't even think to invite me.
3. It felt like a double date.

So, I told him, "Sure, but you're not taking my car."

The moment I said no, he suddenly didn't want to go anymore.

That was the moment I knew—this wasn't just friendship.

As the months went by, I noticed more changes.

Darius suddenly had another phone—one he claimed was just for music.

That was a lie.

Every time someone came near our patio, he would jump and hide the phone. Even when I came around, he would quickly put it away.

And the same girls he met at school? They suddenly followed him on every social media platform.

I started pulling back intimately, because he was changing every day.

March 2019 – My Breaking Point

By March 2019, my anxiety had reached unbearable levels. I was drowning in emotional exhaustion, my body barely holding up under the weight of it all.

One day, I was bowled over in tears, unable to move. I was also struggling with suicidal thoughts.

I was on the phone with my mother and grandmother, trying to push through the pain. Alyssa happened to come over, and when my grandmother heard how bad I was, she asked Alyssa to take me to the hospital.

Darius was right there the entire time—but he didn't seem to care about what I was going through.

Alyssa took me to the hospital and stayed with me the entire time.

At the hospital, they ran bloodwork, a pelvic exam, and an ultrasound. Then, I was placed on a 5150 hold because I had admitted to having suicidal thoughts.

A nurse came in and asked me if I was sexually active and if I had multiple partners. I was taken aback by the question because I was married and had only been with Darius.

I was given a pill to help with anxiety and another to clear up something—something I wasn't even told I had. I assumed they didn't tell me because of my 5150 hold and were worried about how I'd react.

Before being discharged, they told me I could only leave if I agreed to take Prozac and attend therapy. I agreed because at that point, I just wanted to go home.

May 31, 2019 – His Birthday & the Final Confirmation

For his birthday, I made sure he felt good and looked good.

I took pictures of him and our children before he left for school.

Later, he came home and started uploading his pictures on social media. But I noticed something—none of the photos I took made it to his page.

That night, as we were getting ready for bed, I had a gut feeling.

Darius fell asleep before me, and that's when I went through his phone.

I opened Snapchat—and there it was. One of his "sis" friends.

The messages?

- "I love you."
- "Send me pictures."
- "I just got out of the shower."

A picture of him and her on his birthday and much worse.

Lemmesha

I was boiling mad. My anxiety flared up, and I was shaking.

I woke him up and demanded an explanation.

His excuse? He was talking to her "like he was talking to me" to get advice from her about me.

I didn't believe him.

I told him, "If this is what you want, call her. Tell her to come pick you and your stuff up. But leave my phone, because I'm the one paying for it."

Later, I found out he had bought her a ring but never gave it to her—because I got to the mail first and took it. When he realized, he tried to convince me it was meant for me, but I knew better. I had known all along.

Even after everything, he continued talking to her behind my back.

So, I decided to test him.

I made a male friend—strictly a friend—who had no access to my number, socials (just Snapchat), or even my real name.

One day, Darius caught me messaging him and asked, Who are you talking to?

I told him and showed him the messages.

That set him off.

Suddenly, I was in the wrong.

But the difference?

- I wasn't emotionally attached.
- I wasn't telling this man I loved him.
- I wasn't sneaking around.

That's when I began to withdraw from him—both physically and emotionally. Even when I said I was tired or not in the mood, he didn't stop. He would still take what he wanted, and I would just lay there, silent, convincing myself that it was normal because he was my husband. I thought that was just part of marriage. It wasn't until way later that I realized what it truly was—rape. And it wasn't just once; it happened repeatedly throughout our marriage.

June 2019 – Darius Graduates

Despite everything, Darius graduated on June 27, 2019.

A month before graduation, I reached out to his family, hoping someone would come to support him. I even offered to cover part of their travel expenses, just so he wouldn't have to walk that stage alone.

But I was there, our kids were there, and my family was there, cheering him on.

After graduation, he landed a job at Family Dollar. He loved it until new management took over, and he eventually left the same day as COVID-19 shutdown in 2020.

February 2020 – The Ultimate Accusation

On February 4, 2020, I was taking Alyssa to an appointment when I got a call from Darius.

He was frantic.

A detective and a police officer had shown up at our home accusing him of sexually assaulting Aria, who was a minor and giving her an STD.

I was in shock.

I immediately asked for the detective's contact information because:

1. I didn't believe it.

2. I felt deep down this was Aubrey's retaliation.

I contacted the detective the same day, providing them with text messages, screenshots, and evidence showing everything that had transpired between Aubrey, Aria, Darius, and myself.

We never heard anything else about it after that. They didn't even take DNA from Darius because too much time had passed.

But at that moment, I knew—this was the final nail in the coffin.

What made things even worse was that even without DNA evidence, they told Darius that Aria had contracted an STI called PID.

That was another gut punch.

2021 – A False Sense of Stability

The year 2021 started off relatively calm, but that peace didn't last.

Lemmesha

In May 2021, Darius's nephew Xavier was going through some things, so we opened our doors to him and let him stay with us.

A few months later, another nephew, Julian, also needed a place to stay. Without hesitation, we took him in as well.

At first, everything seemed fine—but then, jealousy started to build.

Xavier began resenting, because of the attention we were giving Julian, even though we were just trying to help them both.

The difference was Julian was actively working toward independence. I helped him find a job for the holidays, and he took the opportunity without hesitation.

On the other hand, Xavier was more focused on his relationship than getting on his feet. He kept his plans to himself, and even when I tried helping him, he insisted on doing things his own way—even setting up job interviews without letting us know as we were the ones who was going to take him.

What started as a safe space for family slowly turned into tension and conflict.

October 20, 2021 – The Family Blowup

On October 20, 2021, I was on my way to work when all hell broke loose.

Xavier had posted something on social media that set Darius off.

Darius called me while the argument was escalating, but I was too far away to get home in time.

I yelled over the phone, begging Darius to stop because I knew how he was when he got angry. When Darius saw red, he didn't care who was in front of him.

The situation escalated even more when Xavier threatened Darius with a gun—while my kids were present.

Julian tried to break up the fight, but Isaiah—despite being young—stood up for his father.

Eventually, things died down, and before I even got home, Darius made sure Xavier was out of the house.

The Fallout

After that, my phone wouldn't stop ringing—Darius's family was calling me, wanting to know what had happened.

Lemmesha

But I wasn't there.

By the time I got home, I messaged Xavier to find out what had really happened.

Turns out, the whole situation was a misunderstanding that got blown out of proportion. But instead of trying to talk it out, things had escalated too far.

Rather than making peace, Xavier blocked everyone on social media and started turning people against Darius—even trying to ruin his relationships with the people he had introduced him to.

But before he left, he sent me one last message.

He told me:

"Auntie, you've always been good to me. You've done a lot for me. But be careful with Darius. I see how he operates. He blames everything on you when you're the one doing everything for the house. You give so much and expect nothing in return, but you don't even know half the things he says about you and your family."

After that, we didn't talk again for over a year.

Rebuilding Broken Ties

Eventually, Xavier left Sacramento, but after a while, he returned—this time to live with his girlfriend and her family.

At some point, he started wanting to make amends with Darius.

I pushed for it too, because I'm big on family and didn't want to see them remain divided forever.

One day, I sat with Darius and told him, "You have to forgive him. You need to talk to him."

Darius's response?

"I wouldn't care if he died tomorrow—I'm not speaking to him."

That broke my heart.

I told him he didn't mean that, but at that moment, he meant every word.

The truth was, Darius loved his family, but he was quick to cut them off when he felt betrayed. He believed that his family only cared about themselves and never truly cared about him.

I had always encouraged Darius to reach out to his family, but he often refused because he felt like they didn't care.

The reason?

They never called or checked on him. And when he did reach out, they would either ignore him or not call back.

That hurt him deeply.

In many ways, I had been the glue holding those relationships together.

Darius & His Nephew Reconnect

Despite what Darius had said, he and Xavier eventually ran into each other and were able to hash things out.

It wasn't easy, but after everything, they rebuilt their bond.

Darius also grew closer to Julian during this time.

We never had many issues with Julian, but in the end, he did his own thing and eventually left.

September 2022 – A Setback on the Road

In September 2022, Darius and I were out delivering packages together when our car suddenly shut off in the middle of the freeway.

We had no choice but to get it towed to a shop, where we were told that the issue was a failed engine.

Thankfully, it was covered under a recall for Hyundai, but that didn't make the situation any easier.

While waiting for the repairs, we had to rely on a rental car for a while, which added another layer of stress and financial strain to everything we were already dealing with.

October 2022 – The Month That Changed Everything

October 2022 was the month that shattered my world.

On October 18, 2022, my sister, Amina, passed away. The pain was unbearable—something I never imagined facing." This makes it more concise and direct while maintaining emotional weight.

Just ten days later, on October 28th, Darius and I were actually excited about something—we finally got our car back.

The moment felt like a small victory, something good in the midst of all the pain I had already been experiencing. We immediately called my parents to share the good news, and in a spur-of-the-moment decision, they showed up with Malcom to celebrate with us.

That night, Darius's nephew, Xavier, also came over, like he usually did, to chill and play a game with him. But this time, Darius wasn't himself—something about his energy just seemed off.

After my parents and brother left for the night, I went to bed while Darius and Xavier stayed up, hanging out on the patio.

Eventually, Xavier went home, and Darius finally came to bed and went to sleep.

October 29, 2022 – The Morning That Changed Everything

At around 5 AM, Darius woke up complaining of chest pain.

He described it as a burning sensation, like acid reflux, but he insisted it didn't feel like anything heart-related.

I immediately asked, "Do you want me to call the 24-hour hotline or 911?"

He refused.

Instead, he said he would do what he always did—take ibuprofen and an acid reflux pill to see if it would pass.

I asked him again, "Are you sure? Do you want me to call for help?"

Again, he refused—Darius was stubborn, and he absolutely hated hospitals.

So, I let it be, and I went back to sleep while he went back onto the patio.

A little while later, he came back into the room, waking me up again. This time, he said the medicine wasn't helping.

I asked again, "Darius, do you want me to call 911?"

He still turned it down, insisting he would try throwing up instead to see if that would bring relief.

I told him, "Okay," and again, I went back to sleep while he returned to the patio.

7:12 – 7:13 AM: The Moment Everything Changed

I woke up to a loud commotion coming from the living room.

Immediately, I jumped out of bed and ran to check.

That's when I found Darius, collapsed on the patio floor, his body twisted to the right—he had fallen through the screen door, his sudden plummet catching him off guard.

My heart dropped.

I rushed over to him, calling his name, trying to get him to respond.

Nothing.

He wasn't answering me.

Panic set in, and I grabbed his phone from the patio (mine was still in the bedroom).

At 7:14 AM, I called 911.

The dispatcher walked me through everything—first, checking for a pulse and breathing.

I told her, "I don't feel a pulse, but he's blowing bubbles out of his mouth!"

She immediately told me, "You need to get him on his back—flat as possible—so you can begin CPR."

But Darius was a big man, and I was alone—there was no one around to help me.

Still, I did everything in my power to get him as flat as I could.

The 911 dispatcher guided me through chest compressions, counting with me to keep his heart pumping. She asked me if my door was locked". I told her yes it was.

Then, she told me:

"Stop CPR and go unlock the front door so the paramedics can get in. Then come back and continue."

I didn't want to stop—I was terrified that if I let go for even a second, I would lose him.

Lemmesha

But I forced myself to run to the door, unlock it, and then rushed back to continue compressions.

Watching Death Up Close

Once you witness death up close, it etches itself into your memory forever.

As I was performing CPR, I watched my husband's eyes roll to the back of his head.

I kept pressing on his chest, praying for a miracle, but deep down, I knew—he was slipping away.

The paramedics arrived and took over.

I had called my cousin and told her what happened and she ran over to my apartment as we live in the same complex. The paramedics wanted someone to be there with me besides my kids as they didn't want them coming out of the room and seeing their father like that.

They shocked him four times right there in our home before loading him into the ambulance.

On the way to the hospital, they shocked him again and again, refusing to give up.

The Hospital & The Wait for Answers

Once the paramedics took Darius to the hospital, I knew I couldn't drive myself. My mind was a blur—I couldn't think straight, let alone drive.

The first person I called was Xavier, my nephew, because he was closer to my home than my parents and could quickly take me to the hospital.

I called both him and his girlfriend, but neither of them answered.

I left a voicemail, hoping one of them would call me back soon.

With no immediate response, I called my parents next.

They picked up right away.

I barely got the words out—I told them what was happening and that I needed to get to the hospital asap.

The moment I hung up, Darius's nephew finally called me back.

I quickly explained what was going on, but by then, my parents had already arrived.

They didn't waste any time—they got me in the car and took me straight to the hospital.

The Hospital & The Search for Answers

As I rushed into the hospital room, the medical team was already in full swing, administering a flurry of tests to Darius, their faces etched with a mix of concern and concentration.

They were trying to determine whether he had suffered a heart attack or if it had been sudden cardiac arrest.

I could feel the weight of uncertainty in the air—no one knew what had truly happened yet, and all I could do was wait.

The Battle for Answers – Holding onto Hope

As the day stretched on, the doctors ran every test they could to figure out exactly what had happened.

They ruled out a heart attack and confirmed that it was arrhythmia that caused him to go into sudden cardiac arrest.

That meant his heart had stopped without warning—no symptoms, no time to prepare. And by the time they got it beating again, there had already been a dangerous lack of oxygen to his brain.

They began a CT scan, but the results wouldn't be available until Monday.

In the meantime, the doctors wanted to keep him cold to protect his brain from further damage, but then they realized—

He was already too cold.

Making the Calls No One Wants to Make

Reality was slowly sinking in, but I still refused to believe this was the end.

I picked up the phone, dialing numbers I never thought I'd have to dial.

I called his family to let them know what was happening.

I could hear the shock in their voices, the way they were grasping for hope, just like I was. But I didn't have the right words to comfort them—because I didn't have any comfort for myself.

I kept repeating the same words, over and over, hoping that maybe saying them out loud would make them feel less real.

"They're running tests."

"We won't know anything until Monday."

"We just have to wait."

Wait. Like I wasn't already living in a nightmare.

The Seizures – More Damage, More Questions

That same day, Darius started having myoclonic seizures.

Each one was another blow to his brain as there was swelling still on his head.

I sat there, helpless, watching the man I loved twitch and jerk, knowing each movement meant more damage, less hope.

The doctors said we had to wait until Monday for an MRI to get a clearer picture.

So we waited.

And as the hours dragged by, the doctors made another decision—

They put Darius into an induced coma that same day.

October 30, 2022 – The Days of Endless Waiting

The next morning, I was right back at the hospital.

I arrived as soon as the visiting hours started, and I stayed until the visiting hours were over.

I refused to leave his side.

My parents were there every single day with me, sitting in the lobby while I sat in the cold hospital room.

Our friends who were like family and my family came, offering their love and support in person and text/phone call. It was very much appreciated during this time.

I wouldn't eat.

I lost a significant amount of weight that I didn't even recognize my own self.

I wouldn't leave his room.

I just sat there, holding his hand, crying, trying to understand why this was happening.

I could only sleep while I was there but I would wake up thinking I was missing something.

I kept hoping that he would wake up.

That he would squeeze my hand.

That he would show me some kind of sign.

But he never did.

October 31, 2022 – The Words I Wasn't Ready For

The hospital had run every test they could.

And now, the results are in.

I knew it was bad—I could see it in their faces before they even opened their mouths.

The doctor took a deep breath before he spoke to show me the result of the CT scan and the MRI.

"There's nothing more we can do."

Lemmesha

I blinked, shaking my head in disbelief. All I could think of this is not how it was in the movies.

"The damage to his brain is irreversible."

I couldn't breathe.

"The only function left is his brain stem."

Everything around me went silent.

I felt like I was floating outside of my body.

Darius was not breathing on his own but his heart was still beating.

I turned to look at him, lying there motionless, tubes keeping him alive.

I shook my head, denying reality, gripping his hand tighter as if I could physically hold onto him and keep him here.

"Are you sure?"

I already knew.

I just couldn't accept it.

The Weight of an Impossible Decision

The doctors didn't pressure me to make a sudden decision about removing Darius from life support, but the reality was still there—

A decision needed to be made.

I left his room, barely able to stand, and walked to where my parents were waiting.

The moment I saw them, I broke down.

I didn't have the strength to hold it together anymore.

I told them the words that felt like knives tearing into my chest.

"He's gone. There's nothing they can do for him."

I could barely get the words out.

I tried to gather myself to call his family, but every time I reached for the phone, I froze.

How do you tell someone that their son, their brother, their flesh and blood, is gone—even though a ventilator is still sustaining his body

Lemmesha

I couldn't do it.

So, I asked my parents to make the calls for me.

I still tried to text who I could, but my hands were shaking, and the words on my screen blurred through my tears. I also manage to call my dad and mom 2.

Breaking the News to Our Children

But the hardest moment came the next day.

On November 1, 2022, I faced a moment no mother should ever have to endure—telling our children the unthinkable. Their father—the man they had known, loved, and looked up to—was dying.

But I couldn't find the words on my own.

I clung to my parents, searching for the words I couldn't say alone. But there are no words for that kind of pain.

How do you meet your children's gaze and tell them their hero won't be coming home? How do you prepare them for a loss that will reshape their world forever?

Lemmesha

Saying Goodbye

I led them to the hospital, knowing they were about to say their final goodbyes. It was the hardest thing I had ever done.

Our two oldest—they understood. Their eyes held the weight of it all: the pain, the confusion, the heartbreak. They stood by their father's bedside, holding back tears, whispering quiet words they wanted him to hear.

But our daughter and youngest son… they kept their distance, frozen in uncertainty.

The man lying there—hooked up to machines, motionless—was a stranger to them.

Their father was the man who made them laugh. The man who hugged them tight, who joked and played and lifted them in the air.

But the man before them wasn't him.

And in their innocent eyes, they couldn't understand why Daddy wasn't waking up.

I didn't force them. I couldn't.

I just stood there, my heart breaking for them, for all of us, knowing this moment would stay with them for the rest of their lives.

Support in the Darkness

The hospital provided a social worker and grief counselor for me and the kids.

They stepped in to offer support, helping me set up therapy for the children—because even though I wanted to shield them from the pain, I knew this was something they would need help navigating.

And honestly, so would I.

Because how do you survive this kind of pain?

How do you keep moving when it feels like the ground beneath you has completely shattered?

Darius's Family – A Tense and Painful Reunion

Darius's family didn't want me to make any decisions until they could be there in person.

I understood that. I respected that.

On November 2, 2022, his father arrived first.

I wasn't aware when he came to the hospital, but he had already been to see his son.

Later that day, the rest of Darius's family arrived.

It was painful—seeing them was a reminder of how serious this was.

His mother, father, three of his sisters (Kendra, Arelle, Belinda), two brothers Derrick and Lamar, a brother-in-law, and his aunt Vanessa all came to visit.

But it wasn't the family reunion anyone wanted.

They weren't coming together for a celebration.

They were coming to say goodbye.

November 3, 2022 – The Heaviest Day

The next day, the hospital room was full.

His family was there—his mother, father, siblings, his aunt, his nephew, and his girlfriend.

My parents, grandmother, and my aunt stood by my side.

Even our oldest son was there.

We were all waiting, gathered in a private room before the final conference.

The room was heavy with silence and whispers, the kind where you could feel the weight of what was coming.

Some sat in quiet conversation. Others stared at the floor, lost in thought.

The Family Conference

I allowed the doctors to hold a family conference, so everyone could hear exactly what had been told to me.

I didn't want there to be any confusion.

I didn't want to be the one explaining it, as if it wasn't already ripping me apart inside.

So, we sat together, as one broken family, and the doctors explained the reality and showed Darius's ct scan and MRI up on the screen.

That Darius was no longer there.

That the brain damage was irreversible.

That all he had left was his brain stem.

They asked so many questions hoping for a different answer or reality but the outcome was still the same.

The Quiet Truth

That's when his aunt pulled me to the side.

She looked at me, her eyes full of pain.

She didn't say much, but she didn't have to.

She already knew.

"You have a big decision to make," she said softly.

I nodded, barely holding myself together.

"I already know. But I can't tell them."

And I knew exactly what she meant.

She knew he was already gone—but it wasn't her place to say it out loud.

I was carrying the weight of the decision no one else wanted to acknowledge.

And the clock was ticking.

Holding On – The Struggle Between Hope and Reality

The day after the family conference, Darius's family left.

Before they walked away, they promised me they would be by my side, that they'd come back to support me, and that they'd be there for him too.

But they also begged me to keep him on the ventilator, to not pull the plug, holding onto hope that he would somehow come out of it.

I agreed.

Not for them—but for me.

For my own selfish reasons.

Because deep down, I wasn't ready to let him go.

Torn Between Hope and Truth

I couldn't imagine my life without him.

I couldn't see myself being alone.

I held onto the hope that he would wake up, that he'd open his eyes, that he'd find his way back to me and the kids.

But the truth?

I knew.

I knew the moment they wheeled him out of the house, that he was already gone.

And in my heart, I remembered the conversations we'd had before—

That if he was ever in this position, to let him go.

He had made it clear.

"Don't let me lay in a bed with no life. Cremate me."

But I couldn't do it.

Because I remembered how he grieved his grandmother—how many times he said, "If anything ever happened to me, I just want to be with her."

And as much as I wanted to honor his wishes, I couldn't bring myself to let go.

So, I decided to keep him on the ventilator, at least until he was stable enough to be moved to another facility.

Fighting for a Miracle

Every day, I was there.

Praying over him.

Talking to him.

Researching everything I could, reading things I never thought I'd have to understand, hoping to find some way to bring him back.

I refused to give up.

My parents were there every day, sitting by my side, holding me up when I didn't have the strength to stand.

Elise came too, most days, offering her love and presence.

Darius's nephew Xavier visited only a few times—and only stayed for about an hour each time.

And every day, I kept his family updated. If anything changed, they knew.

The Move to Folsom – A New Phase of Waiting

Before he could be transferred, Darius had to undergo a tracheostomy to help him breathe.

And on November 15, 2022, he was finally stable enough to be transferred to a short long-term facility in Folsom, CA.

I wasn't there when they moved him.

They transferred him after visiting hours, and all I could do was wait for a call.

Later that night, the facility reached out to tell me he made it safely, that they were getting him settled in.

Adjusting to a New Routine

The next day, I was there—signing paperwork, meeting the staff, setting things in place.

But I knew things were about to get harder.

Because before all this happened, I had already accepted a new job—and now it was starting.

I wouldn't be able to be there first thing in the morning like I had been before.

The guilt ate me alive.

Trying to Balance Everything

I decided to stop updating everyone individually.

It was becoming too much, having to repeat the same painful news over and over.

So I told Darius's nephew Xavier, "I'll update you. You can tell the rest of the family."

It was the only way I could protect my peace.

I asked my parents and Xavier to visit him during the day, switching off different days so that someone would always be there.

Xavier agreed but only visited once—just to give his uncle a fresh haircut and shave.

And after that, he never came back.

It was my parents who were there, every single day, sitting by his side, calling me if anything changed.

I worked until 5 PM every day, and the facility was 40 minutes from home.

By the time I got there, I only had about an hour and a half to visit.

But I still went.

Every day.

Learning, Hoping, and Losing Myself

I washed his hair.

I washed his feet.

I did anything I could.

I learned how to do basic care tasks, hoping that one day—even if it took months—he'd be strong enough to come home.

And for a moment, there was hope.

When the seizure medications were lowered, Darius's eyes opened. But it wasn't awareness—it was only a reflex, controlled by the brain stem, not a sign of recovery.

Still, I wanted to believe.

But that hope was short-lived.

The myoclonic seizures never stopped.

And every seizure brought more damage.

The doctors changed his medications, tried to control the episodes, but every test came back with the same devastating news—More damage.

More of his brain was lost.

And little by little, I was losing hope.

The GoFundMe Promise

During this time, his family set up a GoFundMe account to help with his medical needs and expenses.

I accepted the money and kept it in a bank account I barely touched, wanting to be responsible with every dollar.

I wasn't spending it.

I was saving it—Holding onto it, just in case there was anything he might need for his care, or if something changed and it could help bring him home.

Because as much as I knew the reality, I still couldn't let go of every little piece of hope.

December 2022 – The Weight of It All

By December 21, 2022, I had reached my limit.

Trying to balance work and the emotional toll of Darius's condition was crushing me. I was overwhelmed, distracted, and constantly weighed down by the fear and uncertainty of every moment.

So, I made the decision to quit my job.

I couldn't focus.

I couldn't pretend to be okay.

Not when my husband was laying in a facility, fighting for every breath.

I wanted to be with him—fully.

Every moment, every second.

From that day forward, I was there earlier and stayed all day.

The nurses knew me by name by now.

They saw the toll it was taking on me, and they told me, "You need to take a break, for your own sake."

But I refused.

How could I walk away, even for a day, when I didn't know how much time I had left with him?

When the Rain Fell

But then, it happened.

I got sick.

It was pouring rain, the kind of storm that feels heavy and endless.

And as much as it tore me apart, I made the hardest decision—

To stay home.

Not because I didn't want to be there, but because I couldn't risk getting him sick.

He was vulnerable, and the last thing I wanted to do was cause him more harm.

I thought it would just be a couple of days.

A small pause.

But I never could've known how those two days would later become another mark of pain.

Family Tensions

Back on December 13, Darius's family reached out again.

They wanted my permission to start another Go-FundMe—

This time, to raise money so they could come back out to visit.

But I said no.

I didn't want them using his condition for that.

I didn't want his situation to be turned into a campaign.

Not when he had already been through so much.

The Last Efforts to Connect

As the month progressed, his family asked me if I would video call them so they could see him, talk to him, and say words of encouragement.

And I did what they asked. I still showed up for them—just like I always did.

And then?

Silence.

No one reached out.

No calls.

No messages.

No questions about how he was doing.

They disappeared.

And I was left—again—alone, holding the weight of it all.

December 29, 2022 – The Day Everything Changed

I woke up that morning to a text message from Darius's older sister.

She was demanding that Darius be transferred to a facility in Las Vegas, where their family lived, so they could "watch over him"—

Claiming it was because I wasn't visiting him every day.

Then, just minutes later, another message came through—

asking for the phone number of the facility where Darius was staying.

And then, suddenly—

"Never mind."

I didn't even have a chance to respond.

I had literally just opened my eyes when those messages hit my phone.

The Breaking Point

But it didn't stop there.

That morning became the day that broke the camel's back.

Because shortly after, I received a voicemail from Darius's auntie Vanessa—

A message that made me boil in anger. Her words:

"I've been avoiding them… I haven't been to the facility

to see Darius… I took the GoFundMe money and blew it… I quit my job."

"Even though I'm his wife, they were going to do everything they could to transfer his medical insurance, move him to Vegas, and take control."

"She claimed she heard from the facility that the nurses didn't like me there."

"She said I was on TikTok dancing and shaking my ass, instead of being by his side."

"She didn't care what I was doing. I wasn't giving updates. I wasn't there. And if I lost love for Darius, I shouldn't pretend to be something I'm not."

That message was the last straw.

Because everything I had done—every sacrifice, every sleepless night, every painful decision—was now being twisted and weaponized against me.

The Truth They Ignored

I wasn't avoiding them.

I wasn't abandoning him.

I stopped giving individual updates because it became too heavy. I'd asked his nephew to relay the updates to the family—and he agreed.

But clearly, he didn't.

And when I was sick, when I stayed away for a couple of days so I wouldn't make Darius sicker—

That became another strike against me.

And the GoFundMe money?

It was sitting in an account, untouched—waiting for anything Darius might need.

But they didn't ask me about that.

They didn't care about the truth.

They just ran with their stories.

Taking Back Control

That day, I went to the facility and put security measures in place.

No one—not one person—could speak to Darius or receive any updates unless it came directly from me. They weren't allowed to visit unless they were on the list.

I wasn't letting anyone interfere with his care again.

I also reached out to his nephew and told him, "Bring me my house keys and anything that belongs to your uncle."

I told his nephew that he wasn't able to visit his uncle anymore.

His nephew said "I don't care what you are talking about, I'm still going to visit my uncle."

"I told him you can try."

And once he did, I did what I should've done long ago—

I blocked the entire family.

The Disrespect Didn't Stop

Even after I blocked them, they kept finding ways to reach out.

Finding new avenues to belittle me, disrespect me, and question every decision I had made.

As much as I wanted to go off, I was advised to stay silent.

To not give them any more power.

And I didn't respond.

But they weren't done.

Darius's other nephew Julian crossed the line—reaching out to my oldest child, trying to drag him into their mess.

He tried to paint me as a monster, saying:

That Darius was going to leave me, and that's why I "did something to him."

That I didn't perform CPR correctly.

That I went to get a family friend—who doesn't even live in the apartment complex—before calling 911.

My Last Words to Them

And that was my breaking point.

I completely went off.

I told him to never text my son's phone again.

I told him,

"I have video footage of everything that happened that day—every second. So don't ever question me again."

I made it clear:

Lemmesha

I never said I was pulling the plug.

No nurse ever went off on me—like they tried to claim.

It was their family that got into arguments with the nurses, not me.

I told him,

"That's why you're blocked. And trust me—if you thought y'all hated me before, it's about to be worse."

And with that, I blocked him, unfriended, and unfollowed every single member of Darius's family.

Standing Alone

That was the day I truly stood alone.

But I didn't care anymore.

Because the people who should've stood with me,

The people who should've been lifting me up,

The people who should've been focused on Darius—

They were the same ones tearing me down.

So, I was done.

A New Facility, Closer to Home

In January 2023, Darius was transferred to another long-term facility closer to home.

And I was there—every single day.

Even with the weight of working, tending to our kids, and keeping up with the house,

- I still made time to be by his side.
- I sat with him, watching TV.
- I gave him foot and hand massages, hoping to comfort him in any small way I could.
- I catered to his needs, making sure he was never alone or neglected.

I even made him a playlist of his favorite music, so he could still feel something while I was there.

I bought him personal hygiene supplies, new shirts—

Because I didn't want him to just lay there in hospital attire every day.

He was still my husband, and I wanted him to feel cared for and dignified, even in that bed.

The Weight of Watching Him Fade

As the months passed, I saw the man I loved fade away.

He lost so much weight that he didn't even look like himself anymore.

His oxygen levels dropped,

And even though he was on the room air, his numbers kept falling.

I saw it in his body.

I felt it in his spirit.

He wasn't fighting anymore.

April 2023 – The Final Step to Peace

In April 2023, I made one of the most painful decisions of my life—

I placed Darius in hospice.

Not because I wanted to give up,

But because I loved him too much to let him suffer any longer.

His body was tired, and his spirit was weary.

He wasn't the same man I married, and I knew it was time to let him have peace.

Family Tensions—Again

But even this decision wasn't met with understanding.

Darius's family didn't see it as an act of love or mercy.

Instead, they saw it as another reason to question me.

They told the hospice team that I was purposely keeping him away from them—

That I was withholding the facility's address so they couldn't visit.

But the truth was, I was waiting until they could confirm if they were actually coming.

Because this wasn't about adding more drama to an already painful situation.

It was about protecting Darius's peace.

And then they took it even further.

Lemmesha

They actually had the nerve to ask hospice if there was foul play involved—

Insinuating that I had something to do with why Darius was in that condition.

The hospice team was stunned.

This wasn't a conversation about care or love.

This wasn't about making sure Darius was comfortable in his final days.

It was about accusations.

It was about control.

It was about them trying to force their way into decisions they were never a part of.

And while I stood there, already carrying the weight of grief,

Already watching the love of my life slip away,

They were still trying to tear me down.

Still trying to twist the narrative.

May 2023 – The Final Disrespect

Just when I thought things were starting to calm down,

when I thought maybe I could finally catch my breath,

May 1st, 2023, shattered that hope.

I checked my mail and found something that made my stomach drop—

a change of address notice for Darius.

It didn't make sense.

I hadn't changed his address.

And Darius couldn't have,

because he was still in a vegetative state.

I immediately went to the local post office for answers.

They printed out the change-of-address request, and there it was—

His sister's Arielle address.

I was livid.

Lemmesha

They thought they were slick—

thinking they could outsmart me,

thinking this would be their way to finally get the address to his facility.

But the joke was on them.

Nothing ever came to the house.

I wasted no time.

I reached out using a text-now number and said:

> "Tell the person thank you for doing this. Now we're back at square one. Now y'all can't see him. If whoever did it thought they were going to get the address to where he is at, that doesn't come in the mail—nothing but bills."

It was illegal and desperate,

but I was always a few steps ahead.

And their response?

Exactly what I expected.

"You're an evil, petty bitch."

"Stupid bitch."

"You'll get what's coming to you."

"Remember, you have kids too."

They thought they could intimidate me.

They thought threats would make me back down.

But all it did was solidify that I was right to protect Darius—

because it wasn't about love, it was about control.

The Wellness Check

A week or two passed,

and just when I thought the storm had died down,

I got an alert on my phone while I was working.

Someone was at my door.

It was a police officer.

My oldest answered and immediately called me.

Lemmesha

The officer explained he was there to conduct a wellness check—

because Darius's older sister, Kendra, had called, claiming concern.

I calmly explained that Darius was not at home—

he was in a facility,

a fact they already knew.

I told the officer that this was just another manipulative move—

their latest attempt to gain the facility's name and address.

The officer understood and assured me that he would inform them.

But even then, I knew they wouldn't stop.

Still, I Extended Grace

And despite everything they'd done,

despite the threats and disrespect,

my heart still softened.

On May 21st, 2023,

I reached out one last time.

I let them know:

"Darius is coming to the end of his term. If anyone would like to see him, let me know within a week or two."

Only his younger brother Lamar responded.

So, from that moment, he became my only point of contact.

But even then, a week passed...

and nothing.

No one asked to come.

No one made any plans.

All I got were casual check-ins.

"How is he doing?"

"We're planning to gather for his birthday."

It was like they didn't understand the urgency of the situation.

On June 6th, I reached out again.

I told his brother Lamar that Darius's oxygen was steadily dropping,

that they were administering morphine every four hours just to keep him comfortable.

His response?

They were still trying to figure out funds to come out.

Still waiting for a better moment.

Still holding back.

I gave him the name of the facility and the visiting hours.

But days passed,

and still…

no one showed up.

The Day I'll Never Forget

June 8, 2023.

I was up early, getting ready to take my son to an appointment.

Alyssa had my car, so I was at her place.

I had just sat down when my phone rang.

It was the hospice team.

They didn't ask if I was okay.

They didn't ask if I was sitting down.

They just said it:

> "Darius is gone."

And I broke.

I wasn't ready.

No matter how much I thought I was prepared,

I wasn't.

Lemmesha

All I could say was:

    "No, no, no."

I immediately called Lamar to break the news.

I ran straight to my parents' home.

I woke them up, sobbing,

and just collapsed to the floor.

I couldn't breathe.

I couldn't stand up.

It was like my entire soul gave out.

They had to physically pick me up off the floor.

I told them,

    "Take me to him."

When Alyssa returned with my car, we went straight to the facility.

My parents and brother followed behind.

The Last Goodbye

No amount of preparation could have prepared me for that moment.

The nurses greeted me with hugs,

but when I reached the room, the hospice team paused me.

They asked if I was ready.

If I needed a moment.

I said I was okay,

but when I walked in—

I wasn't.

I broke.

I held him one last time,

kissed him,

and whispered,

> "I love you."

Lemmesha

I could see the peace on his face,

even if I felt none in my heart.

My cousins, my brother, Isaiah, my parents…

We all stood there,

taking in the final goodbye.

It was overwhelming.

It was unbearable.

And from his family?

Silence.

No one reached out,

no one checked in—

except his younger brother.

On June 10th, he texted me.

He asked how we were doing,

and about funeral arrangements.

They wanted to know if there would be a Zoom option for those who couldn't come.

I explained that the mortuary didn't offer that,

but if anyone came, they were welcome to arrange it themselves.

June 13, 2023

I received a forwarded text from Darius's younger brother, which came from his older sister Kendra. The message read:

> Hi brother, are you at work? I wanted to see if you can text Meme and check if she has any updates on his service. So many people are asking, so we decided to hold his memorial on July 8th at Liberty Park at 2 PM. Please save the date. We're working hard every day to make sure everything is right. Two of our cousins are coming from out of town to honor him—we want this to be a meaningful tribute.

I responded:

"Hello, I don't have a set-in-stone date as I am waiting for the military approval. If that does not go through, he will be cremated like he wanted in the beginning per his last wishes. But I am shooting for the first week in July, probably the 6th, for his services to be held. Whoever comes can record the services or go live, but it's an additional charge for the mortuary to do it. Thank you."

June 14, 2023

I texted Darius's brother to let him know that Darius would be cremated, honoring his final wishes. I also informed him that the service was scheduled for June 29, 2023, and provided the location. I didn't receive a response, but I continued moving forward—finalizing last-minute arrangements and continuing to write his obituary.

June 16, 2023

I sent another message, giving them the website where they could sign Darius's guestbook. Still, no response.

June 18, 2023

Things took another dark turn. Darius's nephews decided to make a disrespectful song about me and posted it on social media. It wasn't just a song—it was another threat, another attempt to tear me down.

Despite how I was being treated, I still reached out to Darius's younger brother.

June 19, 2023

I sent one final text, hoping to de-escalate the situation. I wrote:

"As a result of this video, I am concerned for the safety of my entire family coming to say goodbye to your brother. Unfortunately, I have made a report, but I am asking you to ask your family to back off."

It was never an indication that they couldn't come. It was a plea for them to behave, to leave the drama and tension behind. This wasn't about us. It wasn't about the hate or the blame. This was about laying their brother to rest with dignity and peace.

But they twisted my words, taking my warning as if I was telling them not to come. That was never my intention, but at that point, my focus was on ensuring peace and honoring Darius the right way.

I reached out to his family, hoping—perhaps naively—that they would come to pay their respects. I remember one conversation with Darius when we started talking. He once said that when the day came, his siblings, his mother, and even his father wouldn't show up to his funeral. Those words crushed me. I told him not to think like that—that they would be there, that he would at least have me and my family, even before we had our children. I never imagined that moment would come, and I'd have to see the truth of his words.

June 29, 2023

The day came to lay Darius to rest.

It was beautiful, despite the pain.

Our friends, my family, my childhood friend—they all showed up to support me and my children during one of the hardest moments of our lives. Moreover, some of Darius's cousins traveled from out of state to pay their respects. It was a moment of love, support, and remembrance.

But his immediate family never showed up.

No calls.

No messages.

Not even to check on his children.

They chose silence.

And that silence spoke louder than words.

The Same Day

As if laying her father to rest wasn't already enough, my daughter was attacked on social media by Kendra's daughter. The messages were cruel, cutting deep when my daughter was already hurting:

- "Why yo mama kill my uncle?"
- "She did not."
- "Yes, she did."
- "No."
- "How you gon tell me? Yo mama even said it for her ugly self."
- "Believe what you want. You have a blessed night."
- "Tell yo mama I said don't speak to my family cause my uncle wanted to leave y'all in the first place."

- "I'm not telling my mom anything. You tell her, since you are so bold to assume something, you know nothing about. Maybe you should stay in a child's place like me and mind yours. Stop texting me."

Reading those messages broke me.

Not just as a mother, but as a woman already mourning my husband.

To see my daughter—my child—having to defend me, having to defend herself, in the middle of her grief was unbearable.

I was livid.

But I didn't respond.

I didn't reach out.

I let it go—for the time being. I had to choose my battles, even though my heart was screaming.

But it didn't stop there.

Not long after, my name and photo were plastered across social media by Darius's older brother Brandon with the words:

"This woman murdered my brother."

The comments were cruel, disrespectful, and degrading.

It wasn't just words—it was a public dragging of my name, my character, and my soul.

No matter what I did or said, I was being torn down, vilified by people who were letting their pain turn into hatred. It was like I was their punching bag, taking blow after blow, not because of the truth, but because of their guilt and misplaced anger.

And it didn't stop.

A month later, I received another message—this time from Darius's niece:

"Change your name. You aren't part of this family. You're a killer."

It felt like I was suffocating.

No matter what I did, they were determined to bury me deeper.

But the truth?

They didn't hate me for what I did.

They hated me for what they didn't do—for the guilt they carried but didn't know how to face.

And I carried that pain in silence, not just for me, but for my children.

September 28, 2023

Three months had passed since laying Darius to rest, and just when I thought the chaos had settled, another blow came—this time in the form of a voicemail from the Steve Wilkos show.

At first, I thought it was a joke.

Someone playing on my phone.

I even questioned; how did you get my number?

I didn't call back.

Instead, I texted the number, thinking it would be nothing.

But it wasn't nothing.

It was one of the team members from the show.

Darius's aunt and sister had decided to give them my information—trying to get me to come on the show and take a lie detector test.

I couldn't believe it.

After everything I had already endured, they were still trying to paint me as the villain.

I told the team member my side of the story and respectfully declined.

There was nothing for me to prove.

The day Darius went to the hospital, they ran every test imaginable—blood work, scans, evaluations.

If there had been even a hint of something suspicious, I would've been in custody that day.

But there wasn't.

Because I didn't do anything.

They didn't want truth.

Lemmesha

They wanted someone to blame.

And I was tired of being their target.

Tired of being dragged through the mud.

Tired of being the "bad guy" they so desperately wanted me to be.

I wasn't going to waste my time—or my peace—trying to give them answers they'd never accept.

The Aftermath of Truth

When the dust finally settled, I stood in the wreckage of grief, betrayal, and deception.

But nothing could have prepared me for the agony of the truth that lay ahead.

I learned that my late husband, the man I had loved and stood by for 13 years, had been unfaithful—not just with random women but with multiple people, including Aubrey and two minors.

One of them was Aria, and the other was a young girl he referred to as his "play sister Nia."

What made it worse was knowing that Aubrey and Aria had broken bread with me.

They sat in my home.

They smiled in my face.

They held my child—knowing the entire time what they were doing.

I felt sick to my stomach, disgusted beyond words.

Lemmesha

I don't condone anything with minors—ever. And to know this had been going on, right under my nose, left me feeling shattered.

Looking back, knowing how fiercely I fought to defend his name, it destroys me.

When the accusations first surfaced, I stood beside him—not out of blind loyalty, but because I truly believed in his innocence.

I poured my whole heart into defending him, trusting the man I thought I knew, trusting that he could never be capable of something so monstrous.

But the harshest truth of all?

Everything I swore was a lie…was real.

And with that realization, my entire world collapsed.

I walked around for years with the word "stupid" written across my forehead—figuratively, but painfully real.

I had no proof. Only suspicions I tried to bury because I wanted to believe better.

But the deepest betrayal?

A year before Darius passed, the one person who knew the entire truth said nothing.

Not a word.

I tried to give her the benefit of the doubt—maybe she was afraid. Darius wasn't the nicest person when angry, and when he saw red, it was terrifying.

But then one day, she made a comment that stuck with me. She said, "I respect marriage."

And I wondered... how could you respect marriage and stay silent?

How could you respect marriage while watching mine be destroyed?

And when I finally started connecting the pieces, it shattered me.

I remember the cold sterility of the hospital room, the weight of my own mind pressing down on me. I had been placed on a 5150 hold, drowning in anxiety so thick it felt like I was suffocating. Suicidal thoughts gnawed at the edges of my mind, tangled with a pain too deep to name.

Lemmesha

But what haunted me most wasn't just my unraveling state—it was the truth they had chosen to keep from me.

I later found out through my paperwork that I had contracted the same STI as Aria. That same day, I also miscarried—something the doctors didn't inform me about. I walked out of that hospital thinking I was just broken mentally, but I was broken physically too. And they said nothing.

It was like I had been robbed of a life I didn't even know existed.

And I was sick to my stomach knowing that I lived in a house where lies were fed to me daily. Where I was made to feel like I was crazy for questioning the truth. Where I walked around feeling ashamed, not realizing the shame didn't belong to me.

I had unknowingly carried that pain, walking around with a disease that silently took my child from me.

But the truth is, my marriage had been dying long before he did.

It started in July 2022, before he got sick.

Despite everything, we still tried to work on it.

We tried to save what was already broken, but deep down, I think we both knew it was too late.

I had already started the process of filing for divorce, though he knew nothing about it.

I was tired.

Tired of the accusations that I was doing something wrong when I wasn't.

Tired of coming home to paranoia and being accused of things I wasn't even thinking about.

All I did was work to provide for our household, yet I was treated like the enemy.

It got so bad that I would go to my parents' house—even though they lived far away—just to escape.

I broke down one day and told them, "I can't keep doing this. I'm tired. I'm breaking."

But I couldn't just tell him I wanted a divorce. I couldn't just leave.

I was afraid.

Lemmesha

I had already seen his anger, seen how he reacted when I spoke my truth.

He never hit me—but he didn't have to.

He punched holes in the walls.

He shattered things.

And one day, it escalated.

He pushed our kids out of the room, locked me inside, and choked me.

My babies were beating on the door, trying to protect me, but they were too young to stop him.

And I knew then that leaving wasn't an option—not without a plan.

He made threats.

Told me if I ever left and took his kids, "I'll kill you."

He said if I wanted a divorce, we'd still be under the same roof, co-parenting.

But that wasn't living. That was surviving.

And I was tired of just surviving.

So, I stayed.

But my love faded—slowly, quietly. It wasn't immediate, but it was inevitable.

Even though my love for him was still there, it wasn't the same. I loved him deeply, all the way through—even when he got down. But it wasn't the kind of love that could survive the lies, the betrayal, and the damage.

And when I found out everything—about the infidelity, the betrayal, the deceit—it crushed me. **It hurt. It broke me.** But it also helped me heal a little faster. Because it confirmed that the love I once had was for a man who never existed in the way I believed.

Because how do you love someone who's taken pieces of you that you'll never get back?

How do you mourn someone you were already grieving long before they were gone?

What hurt the most was knowing I could never confront him, never look him in the eye and ask, "Why?"

I could never hear the words, "I'm sorry."

I could never ask why he chose to betray me, why he broke me the way he did.

And that lack of closure, that silence, left a wound I had to learn to heal on my own.

Even though I've found my way through the hurt, it doesn't mean it's gone. I still deal with the trauma. I still get triggered. It's still hard for me to open up. To trust. To fully believe someone won't destroy me the way he did.

I'm still learning how to have healthy relationships with people, to believe in love, in loyalty, in trust.

But I know now that his choices don't define me. His betrayal doesn't shape my future.

I deserve honesty.

I deserve loyalty.

I deserve love that doesn't hurt.

Closing Chapter

This journey wasn't easy to write, nor has it been easy to live. Every chapter of my life carries stories of love, loss, betrayal, growth, and survival. And while this may be the closing chapter of this book, it's not the end of my story.

I've learned that life will break you. It will challenge you in ways you never expected. People you love may disappoint you. People you trust may betray you. And sometimes, the ones you'd give your life for are the very ones who hurt you the most.

But I've also learned that healing is possible. That strength isn't about never falling—it's about finding the courage to stand back up, even when you feel broken beyond repair. I've learned that it's okay to grieve, but it's also okay to live. It's okay to let go, even when it hurts.

I'm not perfect. I never claimed to be. I've made mistakes. I've loved deeply. I've fought hard. And I've survived more than I thought I could. But I've also learned to give myself grace. To stop carrying the guilt for the actions of others. To release the weight that wasn't mine to bear.

Through every loss, I found a deeper sense of purpose. Through every betrayal, I found a greater sense of self. And through every heartbreak, I found a strength I didn't know existed.

This book isn't about painting a perfect picture. It's about showing the raw, unfiltered truth. It's about surviving when survival feels impossible. It's about standing up when life tries to keep me down.

And though I'll always carry scars, they are no longer wounds. They are reminders that I lived, that I fought, that I endured, and that I won.

So, if you take anything from my story, let it be this—no matter how dark the night, morning always comes. No matter how heavy the pain, there is always hope for healing. And no matter how many times life breaks you, you can always put yourself back together.

I don't know what the future holds, but I know I'm walking into it stronger, wiser, and more determined than ever. I'm walking into it with love for myself, hope for what's to come, and gratitude for all that I've survived.

This chapter closes with peace, strength, and a heart open to the journey ahead.

And for anyone reading this who feels like giving up, who feels like life has hit too hard—just know, you can survive this too. You can rise. You can heal. You can reclaim your life.

Because I did. And I'm still standing.

This is not the end. It's a new beginning.

Reflection on Life Now

Looking back, I realize how much I've endured, how many storms I've walked through, and how many battles I've fought silently. My life has been a journey of survival, strength, and growth—but it hasn't been perfect, and neither am I.

I've made mistakes. I've stumbled. I've reacted out of hurt, frustration, and fear. There were times I didn't have the right words; times I didn't handle situations the best way. But every choice, every misstep, and every moment of confusion has shaped who I am today.

Healing hasn't been a straight path. Some days, I feel strong and certain. Other days, I'm reminded of the pain that lingers beneath the surface. The wounds fade, but some days, they still ache. The memories, though quieter, still echo. But every day, I choose to rise. I choose to fight for my peace, my joy, and my future.

Losing my husband, facing betrayal, and standing against everything that tried to break me taught me more about myself than I ever expected. I learned that I am stronger than heartbreak, deeper than pain, and bigger than betrayal.

I also learned that true strength isn't about perfection—it's about acknowledging the struggle. It means standing back up when you fall. It means forgiving yourself when you don't get it right.

I'm still learning how to trust, how to let people in without fear of being destroyed. I'm still finding comfort in solitude, but I'm also learning how to embrace connections that feel safe.

Life now is about choosing me—choosing my happiness, my peace, and my future. I no longer settle for less than I deserve. I refuse to bear the burden of anyone else's past or pain. I refuse to carry the weight of anyone else's guilt or brokenness.

I'm focused on building a life that feels good to me. One filled with love that is pure, loyalty that is unwavering, and peace that isn't dependent on anyone but myself.

I'm raising my children to be strong, honest, and fearless, showing them that even through pain, you can rebuild. You can thrive. You can become whole again.

Lemmesha

I know now that the hardest goodbyes give room for the best hellos. And though life will always carry its struggles, I've made peace with the fact that I survived it all.

I'm not perfect. I'm not without flaws. But I am still standing.

I'm still learning.

I'm still fighting.

And I'm still becoming.

This is my life now. A life that's mine to shape, on my terms, with no apologies.

Acknowledgments

I am profoundly grateful to those who walked this journey with me. To my family and friends, thank you for your unwavering love, patience, and encouragement. Your belief in me gave me strength on the days when I doubted myself.

To my sister, Amina, your memory continues to inspire me in ways words can't capture. Though you're no longer here, your love and the bond we shared gave me the courage to tell my story. This book is a reflection of that strength.

To every reader who has chosen to embrace this story, thank you. I hope this book brings you courage, healing, and understanding.

And lastly, to my ancestors, for the strength, resilience, and wisdom I carry—this is for you.

About the Author

Lemmesha is a writer, creator, and a woman who has turned survival into strength and pain into purpose. She has faced storms that would have broken most, but instead of falling, she chose to rise—again and again. Every scar and setback became fuel for her resilience, proving that even the deepest wounds can forge the strongest warriors.

As a Black, veteran, and women-owned business woman, Lemmesha is living proof that struggle doesn't define you—it's what you choose to build from it that shapes your legacy. Her words are raw, unfiltered, and a reflection of her truth, her battles, and her triumphs. She writes to empower, to heal, and to remind others that even in the darkest moments, there's light to be found.

This is her debut book, but it is far from the last chapter of her story. When she isn't writing, Lemmesha is creating, manifesting, and walking in alignment with her higher self—focused on building a legacy of wealth, love, and purpose that will impact generations to come.

Preview for the Next Journey

Love finds us in the most unexpected places, sometimes tangled in memories and shadowed by loss. It's not just a love story—it's a journey through grief, healing, and the courage it takes to open your heart again.

Maybe one day, I'll share the raw, unfiltered reality of loving after loss—of finding peace in a love that doesn't fit the world's expectations.

Because love isn't always easy, but it's always worth it.